T0572464

Presented to

My daughter, Susan Schaaff

On the occasion of

Our path of living & learning

From

Mom

Date

Late 2021 & early 2022

©MCMXCIX by Barbour Publishing, Inc.

ISBN 1-57748-648-X

Scripture quotations are taken from the Authorized King James Version of the Bible.

Published by Barbour Publishing, Inc., P. O. Box 719, Uhrichsville, Ohio 44683

 Member of the
Evangelical Christian
Publishers Association

Printed in China.

the Language
of the Heart

Written and Compiled by
Ellyn Sanna

BARBOUR
PUBLISHING, INC.

$\mathcal{L}$ove is the universal language, the language that all human beings speak no matter their age or gender, race or culture. What is more, love is the language that God speaks to us. Love is the embodiment of the Word—Jesus Christ.

The apostle Paul, in his first letter to the Corinthians, tells us how to speak this heart language more clearly, so that our love for one another may be real and living.

We are all pencils in the hand of a writing God, who is sending love letters to the world.

MOTHER TERESA

1

The Only Thing That Matters

Though I speak with the tongues of men and of angels,
and have not [love], I am become as sounding brass,
or a tinkling cymbal. And though I have
the gift of prophecy,
and understand all mysteries, and all knowledge;
and though I have all faith, so that I could remove mountains,
and have not [love], I am nothing.
And though I bestow all my goods to feed the poor,
and though I give my body to be burned,
and have not [love], it profiteth me nothing.

1 CORINTHIANS 13:1–3

We are custodians, keepers of each other's hearts and secrets. We treasure them with tenderness and fidelity. There is always risk when one is dealing with priceless treasures. But we. . .prefer to take that risk.

LIONEL A. WHISTON,
For Those Who Love

*Love is the master key that opens
the gates of happiness.*

OLIVER WENDELL HOLMES

The supreme happiness of life is the conviction of being loved for yourself, or, more correctly, being loved in spite of yourself.

VICTOR HUGO

The Richest of Rewards

Sometimes Christians who emphasize the importance of love are criticized for having a "feel good" religion. But in reality, that's what the Gospels teach us, and the apostle Paul certainly agreed: Love is the message Jesus Christ brought to earth, and without love we can never hope to be like Him.

Love is not easy, though. Love demands more of us than anything else. It asks that we lay down our selfishness, our rights to ourselves, and instead give to another human being. And it also demands that we let down the walls that we use to protect our hearts and allow ourselves to be vulnerable to each other. There's nothing quite so scary or so difficult as surrendering ourselves, either to God or another person. Love is risky business.

But the rewards are well worth all the risk and hardship.

Yes, yours, my love,
is the right human face.
I in my mind had waited for this long,
Seeing the false and searching for the true,
Then found you as a traveller finds a place
Of welcome suddenly amid the wrong
Valleys and rocks and twisting roads.

EDWIN MUIR

[Love] is the divine vitality that
everywhere produces and restores life.
To each and every one of us,
it gives the power of working miracles if we will.

LYDIA MARIA CHILD

2

The Language of Kindness and Long-Suffering

[Love] suffereth long, and is kind;
charity envieth not;
[love] vaunteth not itself,
is not puffed up.

1 CORINTHIANS 13:4

Love is the heart's immortal thirst
to be completely known and all forgiven.

HENRY VAN DYKE

Familiar acts are beautiful through love.

PERCY BYSSHE SHELLEY

A wife is a spiky,
complex creature brought into conjunction
with another spiky, complex creature.
For the rest of their lives they will be working out
how to fit into the small world of marriage
without damaging each other.

JIMMY MEACHER

Loving Despite the Prickles

One winter a group of porcupines were caught out in a storm. As night fell, they tried to huddle together for warmth—but when they did, their quills kept poking each other. At last, frustrated and angry, several of the porcupines walked away alone into the blizzard. "At least," they muttered to themselves, "we can sleep in peace now." When morning came, however, the porcupines who had huddled close together, finding ways to endure each other's quills, were warm and safe. But the ones who had gone off by themselves were frozen nearly solid from the cold.

We're not so different. When we get close to other people, we end up being hurt—and whether we realize it or not, we hurt others, too. It's far easier to love from a distance; loving the people closest to us, the people we live with and work with, our husbands and wives and children, our neighbors and coworkers—that's hard work. We imperfect humans are a prickly bunch. But when we work out ways to get along, when we forgive each other and accept forgiveness for ourselves, when we offer to each other the ordinary duties of our everyday lives, then we find the warmth of true life, the life that flows from Jesus Christ.

3

The Language of Unselfishness

[Love] doth not behave itself unseemly,
seeketh not her own,
is not easily provoked,
thinketh no evil.

1 CORINTHIANS 13:5

*Love is, above all,
the gift of oneself.*

JEAN ANOUILH

Love consists in this:
that two solitudes protect and border
and greet each other.

RAINER MARIA RILKE

Love is love's reward.

JOHN DRYDEN

Changing Our Priorities

*O*ur world uses the word *love* in many ways. No wonder we get confused about its meaning. After all, we say we love ice cream, or we love baseball—and what we really mean is this: We crave it, or it makes us feel good, or we feel excited and interested about it.

Certainly all those feelings can be a part of any love relationship, particularly the love between a man and a woman. But those feelings of craving and happiness and excitement are really just transitory details that come and go; they have nothing to do with real love, the sort of love that Jesus talked about.

That sort of love has to do with being willing to carry a cross. It means that we're willing to give ourselves away. It asks that we lay down our rights to ourselves and protect the rights of another as though they were our own, trusting them to do the same for us. And most of all it insists that we are no longer the center of our world.

I will give my love an apple without e'er a core,
I will give my love a house without e'er a door,
I will give my love a palace wherein she may be,
And she may unlock it without any key.

My head is the apple without e'er a core,
My mind is the house without e'er a door,
My heart is the palace wherein she may be,
And she may unlock it without any key.

FOLK SONG

You ought to trust me for I do not love and will never love any woman in the world but you, and my chief desire is to link myself to you week by week by bonds which shall ever become more intimate and profound.

Beloved I kiss your memory—your sweetness and beauty have cast a glory upon my life.

SIR WINSTON CHURCHILL,
to his wife, Clementine

Once the realization is accepted that even between the closest people infinite distances exist, a marvelous living side-by-side can grow up for them. . . .

RAINER MARIA RILKE

4

The Truthful Heart

[Love] rejoiceth not in iniquity,
but rejoiceth in the truth.

1 CORINTHIANS 13:6

To Love
with Open Arms

Love should run out to meet love with open arms. Indeed, the ideal story is that of two people who go into love step for step, with a fluttered consciousness, like a pair of children venturing together into a dark room. From the first moment when they see each other, with a pang of curiosity, through stage after stage of growing pleasure and embarrassment, they can read the expression of their own trouble in each other's eyes. There is here no declaration properly so called; the feeling is so plainly shared, that as soon as the man knows what it is in his own heart, he is sure of what is in the woman's.

ROBERT LOUIS STEVENSON,
Virginibus Puerisque

A New Reality

Love demands the truth. It asks us to be real to each other, to let go of all the masks we've worn and stop playing the games we've used to hide our true selves. With painful honesty, we open our arms and allow each other to see our hidden flaws and secret sins.

Love burns away our subterfuge. Naked, exposed, we see each other and know that at last we are truly joined to another person. And, when we look beyond ourselves, we find the entire world on fire with the same glowing truth. We are like Moses taking off his shoes on the burning bush's holy ground; we see God's Spirit gleaming in every sunset and flower, ringing out in every voice and note of music, touching us with each soft breath of air or child's hand against our skin.

We can have no relationship of depth or authenticity if we insist there is nothing wrong with us, or that it is always the other person's fault. . . . To refuse to take responsibility and admit our flaws makes the intimacy and love we seek in relationships an impossibility.

REBECCA MANLEY PIPPERT,
Hope Has Its Reasons

*Love alone is capable of uniting human beings
in such a way as to complete and fulfil them,
for it alone takes them and joins them by
what is deepest in themselves.*

PIÉRRE TEILHARD DE CHARDIN

The Fire of Love

Today a new sun rises for me; everything lives, everything is animated, everything seems to speak to me of my passion, everything invites me to cherish it. The fire consuming me gives to my heart, to all the faculties of my soul, a resilience, an activity which is diffused through all my affections. Since I loved you, my friends are dearer to me; I love myself more; . . .the sounds of my lute seem to me more moving, my voices more harmonious.

NINON DE L'ENCLOS,
to the Marquis de Sévigny in the 1600s

Falling in love. . .is a simultaneous firing of two spirits engaged in the autonomous act of growing up. And the sensation is of something having noiselessly exploded inside each of them.

LAWRENCE DURRELL

Love's Truth

There can be no happiness greater than I enjoyed this afternoon with you, clasped in your arms, your voice mingling with mine, your eyes in mine, your heart upon my heart, our very souls welded together. For me, there is no man on this earth but you. The others I perceive only through your love. I enjoy nothing without you. You are the prism through which the sunshine, the green landscape, and life itself, appear to me. . . . I need your kisses upon my lips, your love in my soul.

JULIETTE DROUET,
to Victor Hugo

I was angry because I cared. If I hadn't loved them, I could have walked away. But love detests what destroys the beloved. Real love stands against the deception, the lie, the sin that destroys.

REBECCA MANLEY PIPPERT,
Hope Has Its Reasons

A Truth That's Ever New

You are always new. The last of your kisses was ever the sweetest; the last smile the brightest; the last movement the gracefullest. When you pass'd my window home yesterday, I was fill'd with as much admiration as if I had then seen you for the first time. You had uttered a half complaint once that I only lov'd your Beauty. Have I nothing else then to love in you but that? Do I not see a heart naturally furnish'd with wings imprison itself with me?

JOHN KEATS,
to Fanny Brawne

God, help me to speak
my heart's language with honesty.
Thank You for the wonderful,
shining truth of those I love,
and remind me to always affirm that truth.
And, God, thank You most of all for Your truth.
May Your words of love strengthen me
and show me Your reality.
Amen.

5

The Language of Endurance

[Love] beareth all things,
believeth all things, hopeth all things,
endureth all things.

1 CORINTHIANS 13:7

*H*eroic love—a love that sacrifices itself for the enrichment of the other. . .is often more satisfying than doing something for ourselves. As we reach out to another, our own needs for fulfillment and love are met. . . .The most satisfied, joyous couples are those that have learned heroic love and practice it daily.

GARY SMALLEY,
Making Love Last Forever

*Love is not, then,
primarily a matter of the emotions.
It is a commitment of the will.
God wills to love us, come what may. . . .
To fall in love under God is to
share this quality of commitment with one's partner.*

LIONEL A. WHISTON,
For Those Who Love

The Bridge of Commitment

*W*e live in a disposable world. Where once we learned to make things work, to fix that which was broken, to make lifelong commitments, now we are quick to throw away that which is imperfect and start over with something new. Unfortunately, we tend to behave in the same way toward our relationships.

Relationships are difficult. All too often they are frustrating or even boring. We cannot expect any human being, no matter how much we love him or how much she loves us, to always stimulate us and stroke our feelings and make us feel alive.

But commitment spans the distance over the hard times, the times when we're tempted to start all over with someone new and interesting. When we walk across this overpass, we will be surprised what we find waiting on the other side.

Commitment may sometimes seem like a narrow, undesirable bridge. But on the other side waits a rich, lush land, a land far greener than our sweetest dreams. And if we had thrown away our love or traded it in for a newer model, we would have missed that endless land altogether.

Love That Endures

*L*ove. . .carries a burden without being burdened, and makes every bitter thing sweet and tasty. . . . Nothing is sweeter than love; nothing stronger, nothing higher, nothing wider; nothing happier, nothing fuller, nothing better in heaven and earth; for love is born of God. . . .

Love. . .doesn't look to the gifts, but to the giver of all good things. . . . Love feels no burden, shrinks from no effort, aims beyond its strength. . . .

Love keeps watch and is never unaware, even when it sleeps; tired, it is never exhausted; hindered, it is never defeated; alarmed, it is never afraid; but like a living flame and a burning torch it bursts upward and blazes forth. . . .

Love is devoted and thankful to God, always trusting and hoping in him, even when it doesn't taste his sweetness. . . .

A lover must willingly accept every hardship and bitterness for the sake of the beloved when misfortune comes. Whoever isn't prepared to endure everything. . .is unworthy to be called a lover.

THOMAS À KEMPIS

True love is but a humble low-born thing,
And hath its food served up in earthen ware;
It is a thing to walk with, hand in hand,
Through the every-dayness of this
      work-day world.

JAMES RUSSELL LOWELL

*Make no mistake about it,
responsibilities toward the other human beings
are the greatest blessings God can send us.*

DOROTHY DIX

6

Eternal Love

[Love] never faileth:
but whether there be prophecies,
they shall fail; whether there be tongues,
they shall cease; whether there be knowledge,
it shall vanish away.

1 CORINTHIANS 13:8

. . .our love hath no decay;
This no tomorrow hath, nor yesterday,
Running it never runs from us away,
But truly keeps its first, last, everlasting day.

JOHN DONNE

Love changes, and in change is true.

WENDELL BERRY

Love is supposed to start with bells ringing and go downhill from there. But it was the opposite for me. There's an intense connection between us, and as we stayed together, the bells rang louder.

LISA NIEMI

Rooted in Eternity

Inevitably, our lives are full of change. The people we fell in love with grow thinner or fatter, balder or grayer; they gain wisdom and experience; they take on new responsibilities and gain new interests. In the meantime, so do we. And all the while, the circumstances of our external lives are changing around us as people come and go, and we move from place to place.

If our love depended on the permanence of any of these outward factors, then it would soon wither and die. But true love lives on despite the constant small shifts and occasional earthquakes in our surrounding world. In fact love grows deeper and wider as it endures drought and hardship, upheaval and loss. Changes only make it richer and stronger, for its roots are not in this world and it will continue on into eternity.

$\mathcal{L}$ove is not love
Which alters when it alteration finds.
. . .O, no! it is an ever fixèd mark,
That looks on tempests and is never shaken.

WILLIAM SHAKESPEARE

*Love bred our fellowship,
let love continue it,
and love shall increase it until death dissolve it.*

JOHN WINTHROP,
first governor of the Massachusetts Bay Colony,
to his fiancée

. . . it will bloom always fairer, fresher, more gracious, because it is a true love, and because genuine love is ever increasing. It is a beautiful plant growing from year to year in the heart, ever extending its palms and branches, doubling every season its glorious clusters and perfumes; and, my dear life, tell me, repeat to me always, that nothing will bruise its bark or its delicate leaves, that it will grow larger in both our hearts, loved, free, watched over, like a life within our life . . .

HONORÉ DE BALZAC,
to his future wife, Madame Evelina Hanska

I think a man and a woman should choose each other for life, for the simple reason that a long life with all its accidents is barely enough for a man and a woman to understand each other; and in this case to understand is to love.

JOHN BUTLER YEATS

If twenty years were to be erased and I were to be presented with the same choice again under the same circumstances I would act precisely as I did then. . . . Perhaps I needed her even more in those searing lonely moments when I—I alone knew in my heart what my decision must be. I have needed her all these twenty years. I love her and need her now. I always will.

DUKE OF WINDSOR,
about his wife

7

The Greatest Language of All

And now abideth faith, hope, [love], these three;
but the greatest of these is [love].

1 CORINTHIANS 13:13

For one human being to love another human being: that is perhaps the most difficult task that has been entrusted to us, the ultimate task, the final test and proof, the work for which all other work is merely preparation.

RAINER MARIA RILKE

Intimacy...
the mystical bond of friendship,
commitment, and understanding.

JAMES DOBSON

I am persuaded that love and humanity are the highest attainments in the school of Christ and the brightest evidences that He is indeed our Master.

JOHN NEWTON

Discipline and Joy

Learning the language of the heart is no quick or easy process. We are all so quick to protect ourselves with silence, to nurse our wounded hearts rather than speak words of love. This language is a simple one—and yet we will need a lifetime to learn love's vocabulary.

Why is that? I think because love is not one single fluffy, pastel word—nor is it a slogan painted in psychedelic colors. Instead, the word *love* is perhaps the greatest, strongest word in any human language, as complex as the human heart and as simple as the Gospel.

Love is the word that Christ teaches to our hearts, a word that demands discipline and self-sacrifice—and one that leads us to eternal joy and holiness.

Never forget that the
most powerful force on earth
is Love.

NELSON ROCKEFELLER

When one has once fully entered the realm of love,
the world—no matter how imperfect—
becomes rich and beautiful,
for it consists solely of opportunities for love.

SOREN KIERKEGAARD

For finally, we are as we love.
It is love that measures our stature.

WILLIAM SLOANE COFFIN

The Greatest Work

To take love seriously and to undergo it and learn it like a profession—that is what. . .people need to do. Like so many other things, people have also misunderstood the position love has in life; they have made it into play and pleasure because they thought that play and pleasure are more blissful than work; but there is nothing happier than work. . . . So those who love must act as if they had a great work to accomplish.

RAINER MARIA RILKE